A
Cottontail
CHRONICLE

Tom Rawinski

Archway Publishing books may be ordered through booksellers or by contacting:

Archway Publishing
1663 Liberty Drive
Bloomington, IN 47403
www.archwaypublishing.com
1 (888) 242-5904

ISBN: 978-1-4808-5051-4 (sc)
ISBN: 978-1-4808-5050-7 (e)

Print information available on the last page.

Archway Publishing rev. date: 08/09/2017

Acknowledgments

My sisters Maryanne, Helen, Liz and Cathy gave their sweet encouragement throughout. I thank also Donna Nelson, Cathy Smith, Marlane Bottino, Sara Davison, Peter Harrity, Jim Sterba and Leominster Public Schools kindergartners.

Once upon a cottontail,
Lovely month of May.
Mother knew with babies few,
Hide them well today.

Nestled snug like bugs in rug,
Kits are nursed and grow.
Open eyes, big surprise.
A world they soon will know.

Away from nest, it's Nature's test. Rain falls through the day.
Fur is wet, so upset.
Rain please go away.

Rain is gone, it's time to *PLAY*. Bunny being bold.

Coast is clear, little fear.

A beauty to behold.

Look inside the water can, hide among the lilies.
Take a peek, hide-and-seek,
Peek-a-boo, so silly!

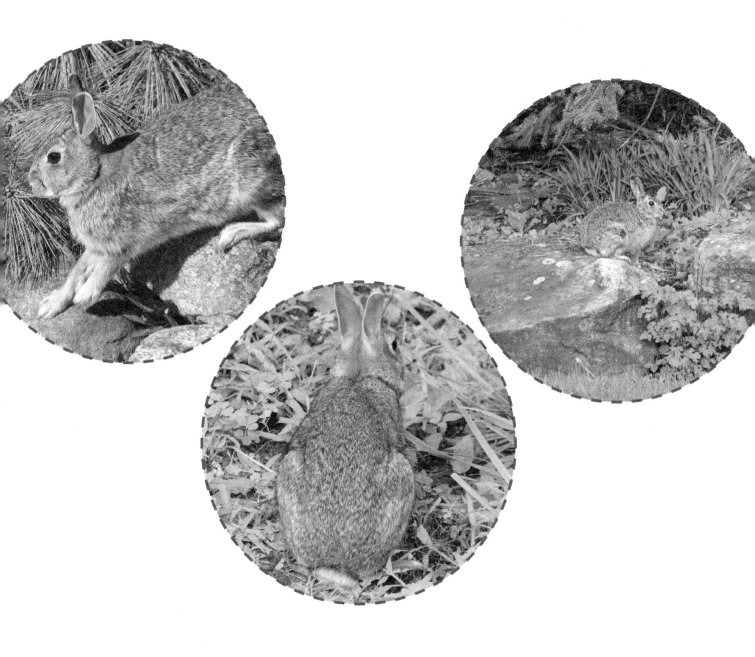

Climbing on the giant rocks, jumping here to there.

Barefoot bunny needs no socks.

Fur her *UNDERWEAR*?

Bunny knows to wash her face,
Keeps her fur so clean.
Dirty toes, goodness knows,
Space with toes between?

Tired now, a little nap.
Stretch and then lie down.
Close her eyes, that is wise.
Napping on the ground.

Doing now what bunnies do,
Breakfast, lunch and sup.
Dandelions, columbines,
Apples eat them up.

The lawn is such a special place, clover in the grass.

Bluets, violets, chickweed too.

Kick the ball to you?

Hungry still, where will she shop?
There inside the gate.
Nibble beets, winter wheat.
Turnip greens are great.

Stand up tall to reach the beans,
The man can spare a few.
Beans are yummy, in her tummy.
Good with morning dew.

Peaches pink with color now,
They ripen in the sun.
Sunset soon, it's afternoon.
Moonlight, day is done.

So much charm on little farm.
Hens are kind to share.
Exploring time, wood to climb.
SNAKES inside of there!

Share the land with feathered friends. Turkey, robin and dove.

Pretty birds, songs are heard,

Sweetly from above.

Father rabbit, proud and strong, hears a distant *HOWL*.

Senses harm, sounds alarm.

Beast is on the *PROWL*!

Coyote on the hunt again.
Dash as *FAST* as she can!
Toothy beast, wants a feast.
WHEW, so glad she ran.

Hiding till the predator is far away and done.

Here at peace, no more beast.

No more need to run.

Play date with her bunny friends, lovely summer eve.

Check them out, all about.

Then it's time to leave.

Chilly till she feels the sun. Winter's on its way.

Frosty morning, it's a warning,

Little time to play.

Winter makes her fur grow warm, she'll seek a cozy den.
Hunker down, in the ground,
And then come out again.

Twigs and branches, chew each one, wishing they were greens.

On the snow, no place to go.

Times are getting lean.

Wintertime she perseveres, shivers through the night.
OWL near, she'll stay right here,
Hidden out of sight.

Time at last the snow is gone, plants begin to grow.

Grass is green, days serene.

Western winds will blow.

Flowers once again appear,
And suddenly she spies?
A nest with sleeping bunnies.
My, oh my, oh my!

THE END

CPSIA information can be obtained
at www.ICGtesting.com
Printed in the USA
BVOW05g0854091217

502385BV00020B/1288/P